GW00359705

Breaking in
your horse

Mark Hallion
and Julie Langrish

The library of Stable Management

Breaking in your horse

Contents

The authors would like to thank the following for their help:
- Malcolm Dunning Saddlery
- Jeremy Mantell MRCVS
- Mrs. Gillian Knight and Mrs. Yvonne Bryant for modelling

Chapter One

Introduction

The art of breaking has been written about many times. This book is based on our experiences in over 20 years of breaking and schooling horses.

The first book in this series, Choosing and Buying your First Horse, guided the first-time buyer away from the young or unbroken horse. To reinforce this, we strongly advise that, if you are a totally inexperienced novice rider, do not undertake the whole breaking process on your own. However, to be involved is obviously the best way to learn. So, if you have bought an unbroken three-year-old, we do urge you to have an experienced person assist you with the whole procedure.

Each year, a large number of horses come to us whose owners have started to break in and for whom things have gone disastrously wrong.

The young, unbroken horse, no matter how long you have owned it or how well you know it, may prove to be a completely different character if you suddenly place a saddle on its back.

Breaking in is not simply a matter of placing a bridle and saddle on a young horse

and hoping for the best. The trainer also needs to assess the horse's character so that he can be at one with the horse psychologically. The experienced trainer knows how much work or new knowledge a young horse can absorb in a schooling session and also knows when to push the horse a little further in its education. Having this ability can be the deciding factor in a horse being successfully broken in.

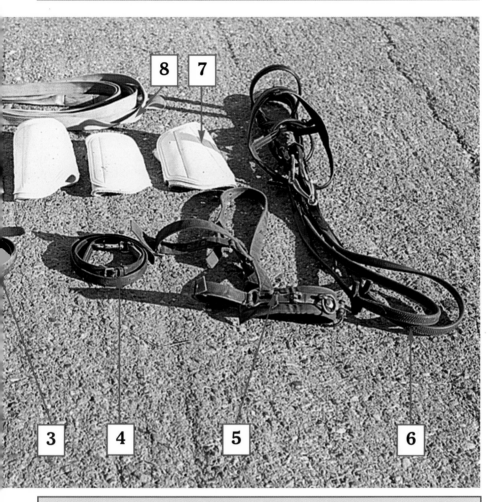

Breaking-in equipment: 1. Lunge whip; 2. Roller; 3 and 4. Side reins; 5. Cavesson; 6. Bridle; 7. Brushing boots; 8. Lunge line.

To the inexperienced trainer, the early signs of a young horse saying that it does not understand or is not confident in something that it is being asked to do may not appear that obvious at first. We will try to help you detect these signs at an early stage and assist you in reacting accordingly.

We begin with why horses behave as they do, followed by handling the youngster, mouthing, lunging and long reining, and ending with the initial backing of the young horse.

Chapter two

Horse
behaviour

2 Before starting out on the breaking procedure, any would-be trainer needs to understand the characteristics of horses, their senses and behavioural patterns. Essentially, horses are herd animals and do appear to be happier when they are in the company of others. A horse that is kept entirely on its own may benefit notably when another animal is put with it. Not only other horses, but even sheep and goats have been known to form close relationships with a horse when kept in the same field.

When a horse is confronted with something that frightens it, either visually or simply by a strange sound, it will often turn and run away. Horses have blind spots and have difficulty in judging distances with one eye. If you are walking around a horse it may not know that you are there. If you touch it without warning, the horse will often jump suddenly and move forward quickly. For this reason, when dealing with any horse and walking around it, use your voice to alert it as to your whereabouts. If you are going to touch it where your hand cannot be seen, first place your hand where the horse can see it, then move it along. It is much better to do this than risk startling the horse.

Horses have an extremely well-developed sense of hearing. They can move their ears in virtually every direction. This is always worth remembering and later, when you are long-reining your horse, you will discover that, although it cannot see you, your voice will alert it to your whereabouts.

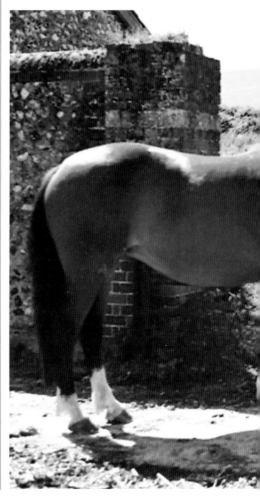

Like people, each horse's temperament is different. Breeding can influence a horse's temperament. 'Cold-blooded' horses, such as heavy horses or cobs, tend to be much more laid back than 'hot-blooded' horses such as thoroughbreds.

Judging a horse's temperament at the purchase stage, looking for signs of bad behaviour, such as kicking and biting, is often an accurate indication of things to come. On the other hand, a horse that always appears interested, puts its ears forward as you approach, is easy to catch and well behaved in the stable yard is generally more pleasurable to work with.

Horses are sociable creatures and love company'

7

Aerial view of Mayhill Stud, the authors' livery yard.

Handling the youngster

 If you have been lucky enough to have owned your youngster since it was a foal and it has now reached breaking-in age, you will be very familiar with it.

More usually, people find themselves with an unknown two- or three-year-old.

Youngsters purchased from stud farms have usually had the benefit of being handled by experienced stud grooms. However, many youngsters bought from sales may have been left to their own devices for their first year or 18 months. Such youngsters can prove quite difficult to handle, and gaining their trust and confidence now will prove particularly beneficial later on.

If you have acquired a yearling or two-year-old that has not been handled, your first task is to train it in hand. At this time, your youngster will probably be kept in a field full time. During the winter, it needs some hard feed as well as hay, and your visits to check and feed it are the start of your handling process. Try to make this visit at the same time each day, and quickly establish a routine. If you feed your horse at a certain time for a few days, it will expect to see you there around that time each day. You will probably find it waiting at the gate when you arrive.

Pop on its head collar and you could reward it with a carrot for being caught, although be careful not to give titbits too often as this is a sure way of teaching it to nip at you. Lead the horse around quietly although make sure you do not pull it along or, indeed, allow it to pull you along either.

When leading, remain at the horse's shoulder. In this position, if it pulls you forward you will be able to hold it back. If the horse does not wish to go forward, it may help if someone stands behind it with a lunge whip to give it a gentle tap on the hind quarters to encourage it to go forwards. However, be sure your helper stands far enough away so that he cannot be kicked. Use your voice; the commands of 'Walk on' and 'Halt' will quickly be understood by your youngster. Once you have taught these simple commands, next teach it to tie up.

Some youngsters react quite violently to being tied up suddenly. When they find that they are unable to walk away, they may pull back very hard. If this happens, the lead rope or head collar can easily break, leaving the horse to run off, probably rather frightened, and very likely you will have a hard job trying to catch it. Worse still, the rope may not break and on certain surfaces the horse will pull back and slip over, which can have a devastating effect on its confidence. Far from making it think twice about pulling back in future, this will probably make it worse.

To avoid any of the above mishaps, the first time you tie up the horse, do so in a stable and stay with it to reassure it. A good idea is to tie it up with a haynet, although never tie it to the haynet itself. Neither should you tie it directly to a tie ring – always make sure that a piece of string is attached to the ring and tie the horse to this. This way, if a horse should pull back, only the string will break, not the lead rope or head collar, and the horse will not end up on the floor.

Now your horse is tied up with a haynet, you can start to groom and attend to your horse's feet. After a short while, your youngster will become quite used to being handled and cared for.

As a two-year-old, the horse can be introduced to the bridle and roller. Great care must be taken with this procedure as a mistake at this early stage could ruin the horse's confidence.

At first, gently lay the roller across the horse's back, with that part of the roller that normally goes under the horse's stomach folded back. If the horse does not object, carefully lower the underneath part of the roller down the horse's side, gently reach under and very lightly do up the roller. If the roller is suddenly done up too tightly, the horse will probably buck and become quite explosive. Monitor the situation carefully. It will feel quite strange to the horse to have something tightening under its stomach.

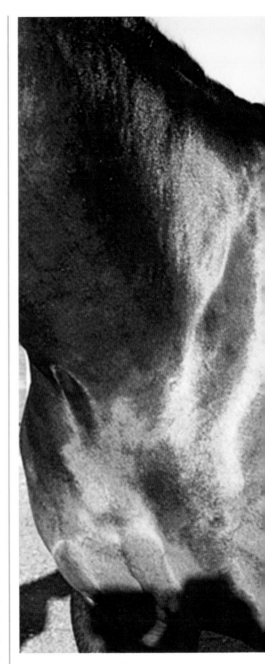

Care should be taken when first doing up the roller.

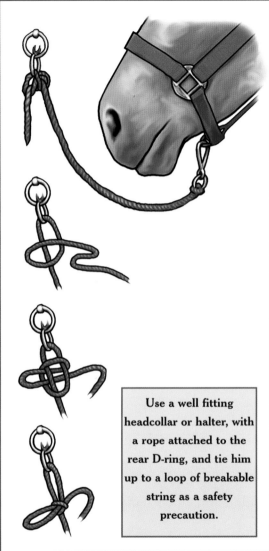

something tightening around its stomach. After a while, the horse will relax and become quite happy about the roller. It may now be necessary to do the roller up slightly tighter. Again, do take care not to do it up too tightly. Over a few days, your horse will become quite used to the roller and accept it as part of the routine.

Use a well fitting headcollar or halter, with a rope attached to the rear D-ring, and tie him up to a loop of breakable string as a safety precaution.

If all goes well, lead the horse gently forwards, again watching carefully that it is not getting worried. Sometimes a horse does not mind the roller being done up, but it might object when it moves off as it then feels

Introducing the bit

We find that a plain lightweight snaffle or rubber bit is as good as any when first introducing a young horse to a bit. Mouthing bits with keys do have their uses, but a youngster's first experience of having a bit in its mouth should be as pleasant as possible.

Before putting on the bridle, make sure that it is the right size. There can be nothing worse for a young horse than to have a bit pulled up very high in its mouth because someone is trying to force the headpiece over its ears.

At this stage the horse can be introduced to side reins, although fitted very loosely, and possibly a small amount of lunging – these two elements of its training are discussed in the next chapter. This is sufficient for a two-year-old; the more serious work begins when it is three years old.

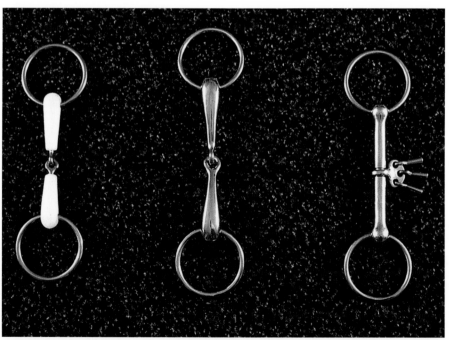

L to r: Light weight plastic coated snaffle. Plain loose ring snaffle. Mouthing bit with keys.

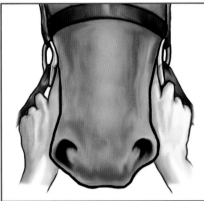

Chapter four

1. Inserting your thumb into the corner of the horse's mouth will cause it to open. The bit can then be slipped into position in one easy movement.

2. Check that the width of the bit is just right by placing your index fingers between the mouth and the bit rings. The fingers should fit snugly.

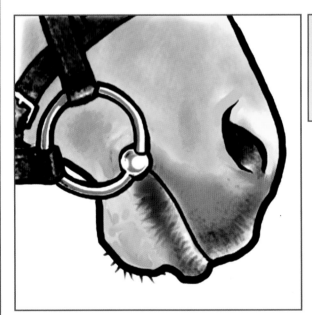

3. A snaffle bit fitted correctly should hang so that the corners of the mouth are slightly wrinkled.

Lunging

 If carried out incorrectly, the inexperienced handler can find early lunging lessons fraught with difficulties.

A young horse suddenly let loose on a lunge rein will not understand what it is supposed to be doing at all. Letting the horse loose on the end of a lunge rein and chasing it around with a stick is definitely not the correct procedure, although many people seem to believe that this is all that is required for a horse to be lunged correctly. You must remember that these lunge lessons are the beginning of the horse's working relationship with a person, and will set the trend for its future attitude towards work and those that work with it.

If you have been lucky enough to have had your horse since a yearling, you will have led it in hand and it will understand the meaning of the words 'Walk on', 'Slow down' and 'Whoa'. It will be used to the bridle and roller, but as a three year old starting out on the breaking procedure, it should now be introduced to the saddle.

A horse used to the roller will usually accept the saddle without much bother. However, when first placing the saddle on its back, remove the stirrups. As with all new experiences, exercise caution and allow the horse time to adjust to something different on its back.

Over the top of its bridle, place a lunging cavesson and side reins. The side reins must be fitted in such a way that they do not pull in the horse's head but also do not allow it to go along in the grazing position either. The side reins are the first step in teaching the young horse to accept the bridle. It must not be made to feel frightened by them. Gradually shorten them over a period of several sessions until the horse can feel a slight contact on them. It is unable to turn its head far to the left or right but it is encouraged to relax its jaw and lower its head and neck (technically known as flexing its poll).

The horse should wear protective brushing boots, preferably with velcro fastening as these are much easier to use on a young animal.

The work in hand should be carried out in the area where the horse will eventually be lunged so that it does not have to cope with any new distractions. The first lunge lesson involves the horse being lead out wearing all its tack, a cavesson and lunge line. You should walk along with the horse and reaffirm the already-established voice aids. During this time, lead the horse from both sides. Frequently ask it to halt and walk on. Continue to lead the horse out for a couple of days, gradually moving away so that it walks out on a circle. Remember to

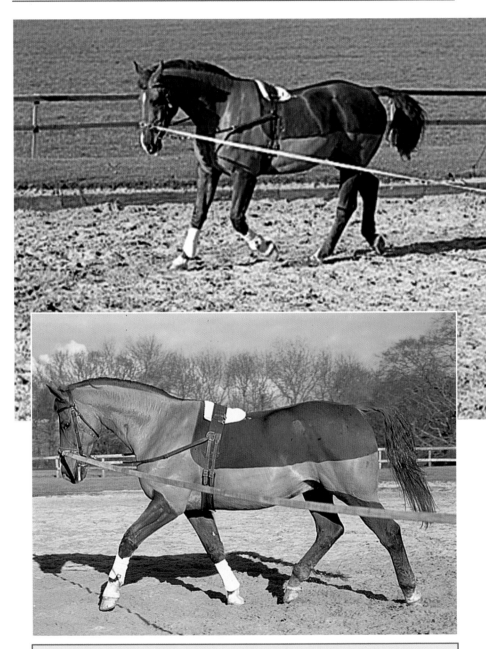

Chapter five

Note the use of side reins to maintain straightness and control.

Author working the horse on the lunge at trot.

alternate between both sides as a young horse will quickly become established on one rein if this is concentrated on for too long. When you are riding, you will need to be able to work on both sides.

At first, do not make the circle much bigger than 10m. Do not rush the horse once it has walked around a small circle and obeyed your voice aids. If you try to hurry the training along, things will start to go wrong. As with all your training, once you have the horse going nicely, end the session

on a good note. Repeat the same process each day, gradually lengthening the lunge line out to a length of 18-20m in diameter. Once you have the horse walking out on a large circle and it is totally obedient to your voice aids, you can begin to introduce trotting to the schooling.

As with the early walking sessions, it is an advantage to have a helper at hand in case the horse is reluctant to go forwards or perhaps intent on going too fast. In the first case, a helper stands between the horse and

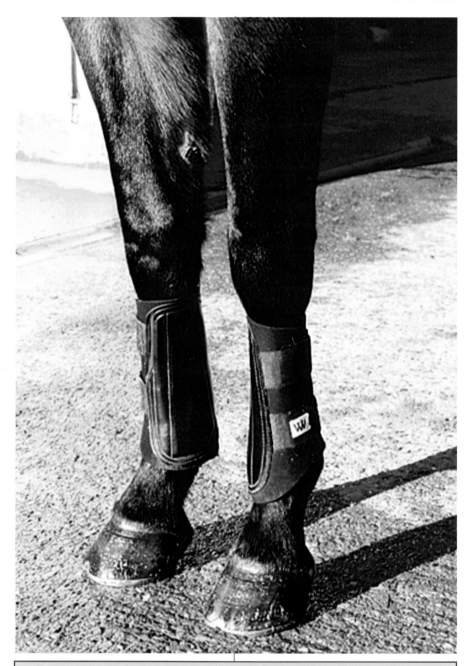

Brushing boots will protect the legs during training.

trainer with a stick and gently encourages the horse to go forwards. A gentle tap just about the hocks usually is sufficient. The intention of the lunge whip is not to frighten the horse but to gain its attention. If the horse tries to rush, the helper can stand between the horse and trainer and hold the lunge line so that the horse feels a little extra restraint.

When you first start your horse trotting on the lunge, he might be slightly unbalanced and find the size of the circle hard to cope with. You can help him by increasing the size of the circle - not by giving him more rein but through walking around a small circle yourself. This enlarges the area and the horse finds it easier to balance itself. Gradually, as the horse becomes more balanced, you will be able to go back to standing on the spot with the horse moving around you. This causes the horse to take up the contact on the lunge line.

These early lunge lessons are aimed at teaching the horse to go on and maintain a good rhythm, balance, co-ordination and obedience. A young horse can do this only for a short time. Lunging places some strain on a young immature horse, so always be on the lookout for any signs of tiredness or stress as you do not want your horse to associate work with either of these things. Bearing this in mind, a lunge lesson should last no longer than 15 or 20 minutes.

As with humans who are either right or left handed, horses have a good and bad side. Never work more on one rein than the other but alternate equally between both.

Once the horse has become established in its lunging, replace the stirrups on the saddle. Let them down sufficiently so that they come to rest just below the saddle flap. Tie them to the girth with string or elastic. Do make sure that they are high enough so that they do not bang on the horse's elbow.

Lead the horse gently forward at first so that it becomes accustomed to the feel of the stirrups against its sides.

Cantering on the lunge should be avoided in the early stages as the young horse finds it difficult to keep its balance. No great harm is done if the horse does happen to break into a canter during a schooling lesson, but do try to avoid it going on for too long. Cantering on the lunge is introduced later, when the horse's ridden work has progressed to the cantering stage.

Chapter six

Long reining

 Long reining or driving the horse will prove especially rewarding for both horse and trainer. Once a horse has learned to understand what is required of it, the long reins will help it to develop a rounder way of going. As the work continues, the trainer will become aware that the horse is getting much softer and more versatile to the hand. As well as developing the correct way of going for a youngster, older horses also benefit from a long-reining session. We find this a very good way of dealing with problem horses that try to evade working in a correct outline.

Long reining is the beginning of making the horse work up to the bridle, and its early experience on the long reins determines and colours its future reactions to a rider's hands. So if you are breaking your own horse and feel that this part of the process may be beyond your experience, it would be wise to get some help from someone with more expertise.

If the young horse has been correctly long reined, when the time comes for it to be ridden it will understand about turning left and right and halting and, later, even the rein back. Riding a young horse that has not been correctly long reined is vastly different from one that has. As with your lunging, the work on long reins must be introduced slowly and correctly. We introduce long reining only when the horse is perfectly happy with being lunged with all its tack and the stirrups let down but tied to the girth.

When the time is right to introduce long reining, first lunge your horse in the normal way. This gains its attention and settles it into a working frame of mind. Do not work the horse so hard on the lunge that it becomes exhausted, in the belief that then it will submit to the next stage of its training without any hesitation. Work it gently until it is concentrating and attentive to your voice aids.

If at all possible, early sessions on the long reins should be carried out indoors or in an enclosed area – this will help to keep the horse's concentration.

Perhaps the most delicate stage of long reining is getting the horse to accept the long rein going around behind it and receiving instructions from the trainer whom it will not be able to see. To start with, the trainer needs two helpers. The first helper stands at the horse's head, and passes a long rein through the stirrups on the nearside to the trainer, who takes it and quietly walks a little to the side and back beyond the horse's quarters. Although he is standing behind the horse it is also better to be slightly offset to one side. Obviously in an arena this will be on the inside.

The first assistant continues to hold the

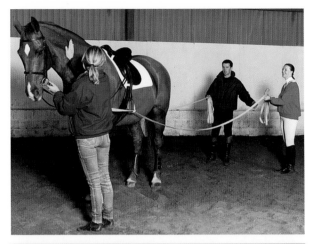

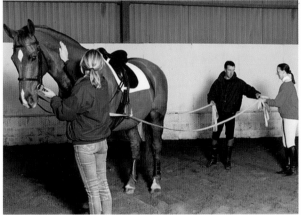

horse, giving it encouragement with their voice. The second assistant passes the other long rein from the bit through the stirrup and very gently walks towards the back of the horse, staying far enough away so that he cannot be kicked. He gives the long rein to the trainer, who is by now behind the horse in the long reining position.

The first assistant is still holding the horse and using their voice to encourage it. Now the horse can feel both reins along its side. It may become a little tense and the helper should continue to hold it. At this time, the horse is focussed on the person leading it, although obviously it is aware that somebody is behind it as well. The trainer should also use his voice to inform the horse of his whereabouts.

**Introducing the horse to long reins.
Great care must be taken to maintain the horse's confidence whilst the reins are placed behind him.**

The assistant should continue to lead the horse until it is relaxed and calm. At this point, the assistant gradually starts to move away. Although the assistant should remain in attendance, the trainer now starts to take over.

As with lunging, the trainer continues to use his voice to ask the horse to do what is required. Side reins should still be fitted for the long reining as they were for the early

Horse accepting the long rein; the author remains a safe distance behind whilst maintaining a light contact.

lunging sessions – not too tightly because the emphasis for achieving the correct way of going, that is, encouraging the horse to flex at its poll and work up to the bridle, now lies in the trainer's hands.

The first long reining session should last no more than 10 minutes. The aim is to get the horse walking gently forwards in a relaxed manner. The same procedure is carried out for several days until the horse is quite relaxed and confident about being controlled by someone standing behind it.

If the training up to now has been carried out correctly, the horse will be confident in its trainer and will soon take to the long rein just as it did with lunging.

Once you have your horse walking forwards, you will start to be able to feel the horse's mouth. Keep everything simple. Work at improving the horse's way of going so that when it is walking it is working actively up to the bridle.

For the inexperienced this may be a little hard to understand. Basically, when you ask a horse to go forwards, you use your voice and, if necessary, a little tap with a lunge whip to make it move. If too much force is required, the horse moves off in a hurried and tense manner. It raises its head above where it should be and this worries it even more. The trainer has to take a strong hold to control the horse which will often make it resist even more. This results in a most unpleasant experience that it will remember.

Alternatively, if the trainer has no contact when the horse moves away, the horse walks

Horse showing some signs of resistance: tense and hollowing against the trainer's hands.

with a flat, inactive step. It has its neck reached out but then lays heavily on the trainer's hands.

Therefore, to ask the horse to go forwards, you want it to move into a light contact with your hands. This balance between the horse going forward actively but accepting the contact on its mouth is what you ultimately require the horse to do when being ridden. So this way of going should be maintained at all times.

When learning to long rein most people do not ask enough of the horse. You should always feel that it wants to take you forwards, not that you are walking along behind it at a snail's pace. Carried out correctly the horse walks along in an outline, accepting the bit in a relaxed and comfortable fashion.

Next, try a few changes of direction. Make these as smooth and unhurried as possible. As the horse turns you should 'allow' with the relevant rein (that is, when turning to the left, give more rein with your right hand; when turning to the right, give more rein with your left hand). Do not, however, give the rein away altogether but, as we have already said, maintain a light receptive contact on the horse's mouth. As your horse becomes more accustomed to walking up to the bridle in an active manner, you will start to feel that the contact on the reins becomes softer and more elasticated. The horse becomes more sensitive to the aids. These signs indicate that the horse's mouth is developing correctly.

As the horse progresses, try long reining a large figure-of-eight but do remember never to pull it around the changes of direction. If this happens you are probably asking it to turn too sharply.

As your long reining progresses, make the work more varied. Work in the school or field. When very experienced at long reining, and if the facilities are available, long reining out on farm tracks is a wonderful experience for a young horse. However, this should be undertaken only by very experienced trainers – inexperienced handlers should remain in the confines of a field or school.

Your horse will now be working well on the lunge and on the long rein. It will be balanced, co-ordinated and attentive to your voice aids. It will be working in an outline with a confident acceptance of the bit. Over the weeks it will have gained confidence and trust in you and has now have reached the stage where it can be backed.

The backing

The backing procedure begins when the horse is lunging correctly.

At the end of a successful lunging or long reining session take the horse back into the stable. You need an assistant to hold the horse, not by the bit but by a lunge line attached to the cavesson. Use a mounting block and lay your weight across the saddle. At first the horse will probably be a little tense and you should not try to lean too far across it. Repeat this action many times until the horse accepts it as part of its normal routine. If the horse should become slightly worried, give it a few minutes to relax and try again. Remember always to finish any training session on a good note.

If you follow this procedure, on the day when you actually take up a normal seat, the horse is thoroughly prepared. When the time is right, take the normal seat position, either by mounting from the block or by having a leg-up. Once there, remain in the saddle for a few minutes. Continue to use your voice to reassure the horse and then dismount. Repeat this four or five times. The horse should be quite calm but if a problem does occur go back a stage and lean across its back. Do not soldier on regardless at this point. If you try to mount the horse and it is not mentally confident it could end up depositing you on the ground. This setback will take a long time to rectify, so do not be impatient. If the horse does not relax and does not let you mount it, go back to laying across its back a few times, then put it away and try again later in the day. By not rushing to get on it, you will eventually be successful; some horses just take a little more time than others to accept the rider's weight.

Assuming you have managed to take up the correct seat, your helper should lead the horse around the stable. Being in the confines of a stable is much safer than trying to mount in an outdoor school. The horse should be backed and ridden in the stable each day for three or four days before you venture outside.

It is always best to use a mounting block for getting on the horse when you mount it outside the stable. In this way, there is less chance of the saddle slipping and it also reduces the pressure on the horse's back. Obviously, at some stage the horse will need to be mounted from the ground, but try to avoid this at first. Using the mounting block also avoids the girth having to be done up too tightly to start with, and is thus much more comfortable for the young horse.

When mounting outside, the horse should be held by a helper with the lunge line attached to a cavesson fitted over the bridle. The helper leads the horse around.

At this stage, the horse will pay more attention to the handler than to the rider. Follow this procedure for a few days, after which the helper should release the lunge line but continue to walk along beside the horse. Gradually, the helper moves away, thereby transferring control to you, the rider. You should always continue to use your voice to back up any aids that you may apply. These voice aids are very familiar to the horse by now. It will be confident in their meaning and at this stage the horse needs as much confidence from the rider as possible.

The early backing of the youngster should be carried out preferably by someone not very heavy and who is relaxed and calm. The horse will be tense and perhaps slightly anxious in the early stages of backing. A person with the above characteristics will gain a horse's acceptance of carrying a rider

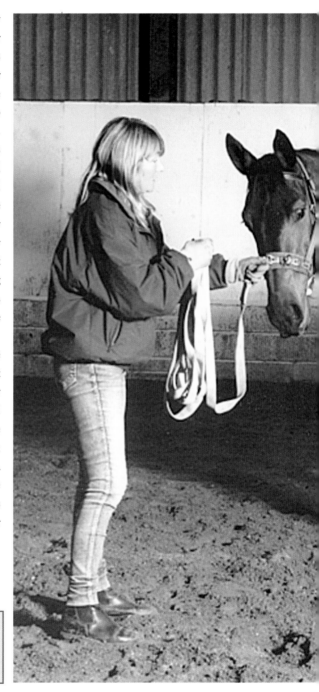

Horse appears relaxed and happy, a sign that he has accepted the early training.

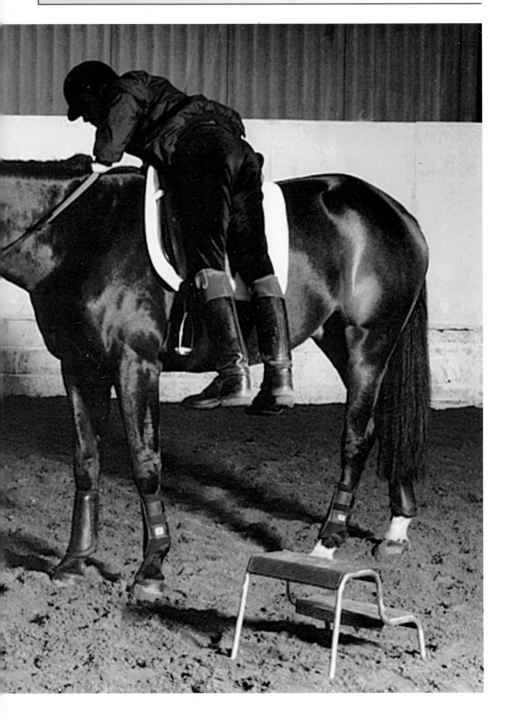

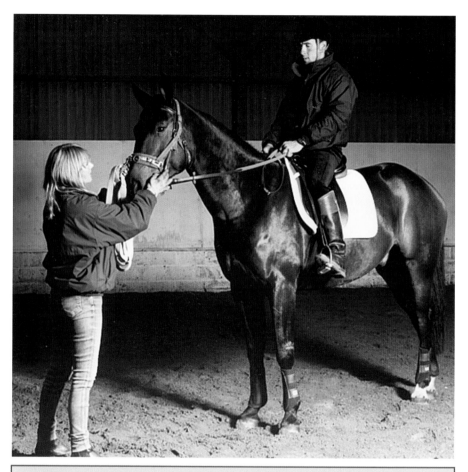

Mission accomplished. Horse happily accommodating the rider's weight.

much more quickly than someone who is afraid that the worst is about to happen.

Your initial breaking and backing is complete. The basics of what you have covered have prepared your horse for its initial ridden work.

Lunging and long reining have given it some balance and a correct way of going. What it goes on to learn now will influence its ridden and competitive career, perhaps for the rest of its life.

30

Glossary

Backing or breaking	-	Training the horse to accept a rider
Bit	-	Used to control the horse from his mouth. Various types are available. Different designs determine the severity of the bit
Bridle	-	The Bridle fits on the horse's head and is connected to the reins and bit
Brushing boots	-	Available in many designs and materials. Designed to protect the horse's lower leg from damage (that is, being struck by another leg)
Cavesson	-	Used when lungeing. Similar to a head collar, it can be fitted over a bridle and allows the trainer to use a ring fitted in the front from which to lunge
Contact	-	The association between the horse and the rider's hand, whether through lunging, long reining or riding
Girth	-	This item of tack secures the saddle to the horse. Either leather or synthetic material is used. The girth is attached to both sides of the saddle and runs under the horse's stomach
Head collar	-	This is a harness which fits over the horse's head, allowing it to be lead
Hocks	-	The hocks are found on the horse's back legs; they are easily recognisible as the point where the lower and upper hind legs meet
Long reining	-	The use of two long reins to control the horse from behind. It introduces the horse to turns and halts and is a preliminary to riding the horse from the saddle
Lunging	-	Lunging involves the horse being attached to a long line and being controlled on a circle by a trainer. The horse is encouraged to move around the trainer, learning to understand the voice commands as well as developing a balance and rhythm to his paces
Lunge whip	-	A long whip which is used to gently encourage a horse to go forward when being lunged or long reined
Mounting block	-	A suitable structure from which the rider can mount a horse without exerting too much pressure on the horse's back
Mouthing	-	Introducing a bit to the horse's mouth, allowing him to become used to the feeling of a piece of metal in his mouth
Outline	-	The visual manner in which a horse carries itself. When ridden in a correct manner, the head and quarters will lower and the neck will become rounded. Correct outline can only be achieved by experienced handling and good schooling
Poll	-	The area just behind the horse's ears. When the horse is in a correct outline, the poll will appear to be the highest point of the horse
Quarters	-	The back part of the horse, the area behind the saddle

Index